A Heart for Reconciliation

A Walk Through 2 Corinthians

Megan Dosher Hansen
and Michael Rinehart

Megan wrote the daily devotions. Mike wrote the background material and the discussion questions for groups.

Thanks to Andrea Martinez, Rebecca McDonald and John Turnquist for their help in reading and editing.

Contents

Discussion Questions for Small Group Gatherings:

Introduction to 2 Corinthians

We have spoken frankly to you Corinthians;
our heart is wide open to you.

—2 Corinthians 6:11

Paul talks a lot about the heart. In 2 Corinthians, Paul uses the word "heart" fourteen times in just 13 chapters. "Heart" appears in each of the first eight chapters. In the midst of a conflict, Paul models open, honest conversation, with a heart that is "wide open." Paul has learned how to have an open heart for reconciliation, a trait we could all use today, as individuals, churches and nations.

2 Corinthians is one of many letters that Paul wrote to the church in Corinth, a city in Greece.

1. **The Warning Letter:** In 1 Corinthians 5:9 says, "I have written you in my letter..." So we know Paul wrote a letter prior to 1 Corinthians. This is sometimes called the "warning letter."
2. **1 Corinthians:** Then we have 1 Corinthians.
3. **The Severe Letter.** In 2 Corinthians 2:3-4 and 7:8, Paul refers to an earlier "letter of tears." 1 Corinthians clearly does not match that description; so this "letter of tears" may have been written between 1 Corinthians and 2 Corinthians.
4. **2 Corinthians.** Refers to the Severe Letter and mends fences.

Reading a letter is like listening to one side of a phone conversation. You have to guess what the other person is saying. It can be a bit of a puzzle. But there are also many things that can be learned, especially regarding way the apostle Paul lived out his theology in the real world of relationships.

A Heart for Reconciliation will give you daily readings as you walk through 2 Corinthians. Begin by reading all of 2 Corinthians in one sitting. This is the best way to get a feel for the scope of the whole letter.

Then read roughly a half of a chapter each day. Each chapter's subheading has a recommended reading for the day. 2 Corinthians has 13 chapters, so this will take about a month. There are 25 chapters in this book. We recommending worship on the first day of the week, and then reading the remaining six days. You'll complete the book in about four weeks.

In the back are some discussion questions for group gatherings. These discussions revolve around five passages from 2 Corinthians, from chapters 4, 5, 6, 8 and 12. Why not gather a group to walk through 2 Corinthians together, or use it as a congregational study?

In addition to the daily readings and weekly discussions in this book, there are also some background materials that can be found at http://bishopmike.com/2-corinthians.

We hope that in walking through 2 Corinthians you will find your heart wide open to God and neighbor.

1

Suffering and Compassion

2 Corinthians 1:1-11

*Blessed be the God and Father of our Lord Jesus Christ,
the Father of mercies and the God of all consolation,
who consoles us in all our affliction, so that we may be able to
console those who are in any affliction with the consolation
with which we ourselves are consoled by God.*

—2 Corinthians 1:3-4

This is a letter between people who know each other well. 2 Corinthians may be Paul's fourth letter to the church in Corinth, a city in Greece. It doesn't read like a formal letter of strangers with common interests, or even of acquaintances, but, rather, it is a very intimate letter. We will see Paul refer to his love and open heart for the Corinthians several times throughout the letter, and here, after a brief greeting, he immediately gets into serious matters. One would not talk to mere acquaintances about the struggles, affliction and humiliation Paul shares here. He seems to not only trust in the friendship shared with the Corinthians, but also that they will understand what he is going through. At the writing of this letter, the Corinthians do not seem to be suffering for their faith in the acute ways Paul has. Paul is keenly aware that the more faithful the Corinthians become, as the church in Corinth grows, the potential for persecution would become greater.

Paul encourages the Corinthians to grow in their faith, to stay with true teachings, not just following the latest, flashiest teachers in town, and to open their hearts, to him and to one another. Paul knows that it is through these things that the love and life of Jesus will remain strong among the Corinthian church, and when persecution, failure and humiliation come, they will be able to continue to trust in God and in one another, knowing that truth and love are more powerful than any suffering. In order to do this, however, they must not give in to petty conflicts or split into factions based on this teaching or that.

Living in the United States, we are not subjected to persecution because of our faith in Jesus Christ (despite a few, loud voices on the internet), so we may not truly understand or experience what Paul describes, twice in this letter. In fact, sometimes the worst suffering we experience as Christians in this country is not inflicted by non-believers, but rather from our own communities. Sadly, sometimes church members can be very hard on one another. This concerns Paul.

As you read this letter, take Paul's advice to heart – to go deeper in faith, to continue to stand up for and follow truth and to build stronger community in order to prevent the types of small-minded, petty arguments that do so much harm to other members of the Body of Christ.

Reflect: Think about your own church community – whom do you think of when you think of people with strong faith? Who do you turn to when you are struggling or life seems to be falling apart? Who turns to you?

HBC small group leaders + the group of sisters in Christ.

2

God's "Yes"

Corinthians 1:12-24

Was I vacillating when I wanted to do this? Do I make my plans according to ordinary human standards, ready to say "Yes, yes" and "No, no" at the same time? ...For in him every one of God's promises is a "Yes." For this reason it is through him that we say the "Amen," to the glory of God.

— 2 Corinthians 1:17, 20

Recently, a blog post was being passed around about RSVPs to invitations (or the lack thereof), a perennial topic of debate. It's one of those subjects everyone loves to complain about – how people fail to respond to RSVPs, then call the day of the event, or just show up – how parents aren't teaching their children manners, and that modern technology is making us careless of each other's time. In the very opening of this letter to the Corinthians, Paul perfectly demonstrates that the issues we think of as being caused by modernity's "busyness" are not new at all, but rather that vacillation and over-promising are both deeply human, and deeply hurtful to friendships. These things are not new. They are part of ordinary life. We all seem ready to say, "Yes, yes," to so many things, while not actually being able to follow through on all of them.

Paul alludes to the very human tendency toward vacillation in the opening of this letter. The Corinthians are unhappy that Paul did not return to Corinth after visiting Macedonia as he had promised. Paul says he is not someone who simply and thoughtlessly says, "Yes," to every request, really having no intention to follow through. He absolutely intends to visit, no matter what it takes. His word means something, more so because it is not just his word and promise, but by his living in accordance with God's word, it is God's word also. Paul also points out (several times in the letter) that he has not abandoned them, but rather sent one of his most beloved and trusted disciples and colleagues, Titus. Sending Titus was not a poor substitute for Paul. It was Paul sending his own heart to the Corinthians, since he could not send his whole body.

Paul wants the Corinthians understand his deep love for and commitment to them. He is also concerned about their propensity for following other charismatic and possibly misleading Christian evangelists, and for slipping back into old, non-Christian ways. Paul is gently reminding them that they, too, have these very human tendencies to say yes and no at the same time. He does not want the Corinthians to say, "Yes, yes," to Christianity and especially Paul's teachings, if their hearts will easily follow every slick-tongued teacher who comes to town. Paul speaks of God's "Yes," which is the true promise, seen in the life of Jesus. What God promises happens. And so, as a man of God's word, Paul, too, will fulfill his promises.

This is the same tendency we have to fight every day, to not say yes to every little thing that catches our eye. If we belong to God and are living into God's "Yes," then we will believe what we do and say has true meaning, that God is in what we do and say. In order to live into that "Yes," we have to know what we believe, and make that the foundation for everything we do. When we do this well, we make commitments of our time to what is truly important – family, friends, people in need, paid and unpaid work, doing things that will better the world, and not simply adding to bank accounts or résumés. Maybe we're not at the hottest parties in town with the most glamorous people, but we find ourselves instead spending time with people we love, and being fulfilled in every thing we do, because they fit who we are, and what we believe as truth. And then we are truly living out and experiencing God's "Yes" in our lives.

Reflect: How would your life change if you said yes and meant it every time? What are the things that distract you from your commitments? What does God's "Yes" look like in your life?

3

Forgiveness

2 Corinthians 2:1-11

Anyone whom you forgive, I also forgive.
What I have forgiven, if I have forgiven anything, has been for your
sake in the presence of Christ.

—2 Corinthians 2:10

In 2 Corinthians 2:1-11 we are offered a powerful picture of Christian forgiveness. Paul references an incident with a particular member of the Corinthian church, one that perhaps led to the previous visit being "painful." We do not know what the offense was, but we do know the community meted out seems to have come to completion, and forgiveness offered to the offender.

When an offense has been truly painful, forgiveness is not just a momentary action speaking words of peace and restoring a person to the community, but an on-going action of remembering to love, to not let the previous offense be punished again and again and it is an action of the whole body. As Paul says in 1 Corinthians 12:26, "If one member suffers, all suffer together with it; if one member is honored, all rejoice together with it." This is reiterated in 2 Corinthians 1:5-7. Just as the suffering and consolation of Christ benefit the whole body, likewise the suffering or consolation of any member is the suffering or consolation of the whole.

Paul speaks of his suffering as being beneficial to the whole body of believers. But he also says that when any individual or particular community in the body suffers, as the Corinthians had, then he also suffers. Paul says forgiveness and comfort work in the same way. If the community decides to forgive and reinstate a member to the body, then Paul, too, will extend forgiveness and love toward that member.

Wow! It is hard enough to get a whole group of people to agree on a restaurant, much less to forgive someone who has done something terrible that hurts the community. Even more so, to be far away from the group when that person is changing, as Paul was, so you remember the pain that person caused without also seeing the transformation. To offer up forgiveness, as Paul does, is not an easy thing. Think about a time when you got angry with someone who hurt a friend or family member. If the person apologizes to your loved one, but you are not there to see it, you probably will remain angry on behalf of the person close to you, even if they are no longer upset.

Overcoming your anger even if you haven't seen redemption is difficult. Of course, we are called to forgive even when we are not asked for forgiveness, and this is part of that practice. Practice, practice, practice is what is required for faithful forgiveness. We humans will keep messing up, keep hurting those we love, and needing forgiveness. We will keep getting hurt by others and needing to offer forgiveness. Paul knew he couldn't get any work done, especially since his work was sharing the life-giving love of Christ, as long as he was holding onto resentments and anger every time he or the people he loved throughout his travels were hurt.

Paul wants to forgive the redeemed offender along with the Corinthians so that when he does visit, he will be acting as one with the whole community. His message is that no matter the distance, the community is one in love and deed.

Reflect: Paul lays out a tough task for us today in a Christian body that has splintered over who can be ordained, who can be married, how we worship, and even which translation of the Bible is "correct." How can we act as one with Christians who we have hurt, or who have hurt us? Who are struggling to forgive? What would it look like to forgive that person?

4

The "Aroma" of Christ

2 Corinthians 2:12-17

*For we are the aroma of Christ to God among those who are being
saved and among those who are perishing; to the one a fragrance
from death to death, to the other a fragrance from life to life.*

—2 Corinthians 2:15-16a

Can you think of a smell that might smell wonderful to one person,
evoking images of home and safety, while to another person
smelling repulsive? The aroma of Paul's ministry smells like life to
some, and like death to others.

Pauls' words seem harsh when he says that as the aroma of Christ to
God, we will be to some a fragrance from "life to life," and to others,
from "death to death." Isn't the good news for everyone? Isn't the
love and resurrection of Christ for everyone? Of course it is, but to
some, the good news is not good.

There are those in the world who believe their status, money and
power mean they are better than others. They deserve everything
they have. Some people believe sacrificing everything for the love of
others, especially of people who have done terrible things, as Jesus
did, is to be weak. To ask for forgiveness and to forgive others is
also to show weakness. If Jesus died for all, if Jesus became weak to
save the weak, then what good are money, influence and strength?
None of those things can buy you the love of Jesus.

The strength of God is exhibited in ways that many people call
weak: forgiving others instead of wreaking vengeance; becoming
human to show love, including being open and vulnerable in ways

that people could get close to, and even hurt God; sacrificing everything, including life itself, for others – all of these things are seen as weak and foolish by so many, including people who call themselves Christians. When it comes to the good news that Christ died for us and that we are to follow in Christ's footsteps, well, that doesn't always seem like such good news. *We* don't want to give up everything for others. *We* don't want to become, or even seen as being, weak and vulnerable.

For those who believe that they have created their success by themselves, without support of others or providence, the good news is death. Death to all they hold dear. They cannot see the life that comes after that death. They simply see and smell the decay of all the things that could never last forever anyway.

Reflect: What things have had to die in you that you might find life? To what things are you clinging now? Which of Jesus' commands challenges you the most?

5

Letters of Christ

2 Corinthians 3:1-11

You yourselves are our letter, written on our hearts, to be known and read by all; and you show that you are a letter of Christ, prepared by us, written not with ink but with the Spirit of the living God, not on tablets of stone but on tablets of human hearts.

—2 Corinthians 3:2-3

The stories we share from the Bible, of God's works from the beginning of creation, are important. They tell us about who this God is, and how we might follow and be like the God who made us. We recognize ourselves in the people throughout Scripture. But without the living body of Christ continuing this story today, these words are nothing more than myths of a distant past, dreams of a people long gone. These words continue to have importance because they continue to be lived out. The kingdom of God continues to sprout and grow in the midst of a broken world through our lives. As Paul says, we could have the most glowing letters of recommendation, but it is the people we touch who really tell our story.

Paul, of course, writes letters all the time, including letters of recommendation, sent along with colleagues such as Timothy and Titus, to introduce them to churches Paul has started. It is because of these letters that we have any of Paul's teachings left to share today. The letters we have are encouraging and life-giving, but as far as the Corinthians were concerned, Paul says they should have no need for further letters of recommendation for his teachings, for they have met him, have gotten to know him, learned his teachings, all in person. Likewise, they should have no need for letters of recommendation to new believers because the Corinthians themselves *are* the letters that show Paul's teachings to be true. They are true because they are Christ's words, not Paul's words.

It was through the Corinthians' words and actions of love and generosity toward one another and non-believers that told the living story of Christ. As we go into the world each day, we are the same – living letters from God in other people's lives. When we see other's gifts and passions, we can encourage them. When someone needs a helping hand, we can stop what we are doing and answer the need in front of us. If someone needs to talk, we can listen. When someone is in despair, we might be a presence of peace and hope. These spell out the simple words of love in the world. And through these words, others might be able to share them with all the people they meet.

Reflect: If your life is a letter of Christ to the world, what does it say? Who is receiving this letter? Who acts as a letter from Christ to you? What messages are those living letters sharing with you?

6

A Bold Hope

2 Corinthians 3:12-4:6

*Since, then, we have such a hope, we act with great boldness...
And all of us, with unveiled faces, seeing the glory of the Lord as
though reflected in a mirror, are being transformed into the same
image from one degree of glory to another; for this comes from the
Lord, the Spirit.*

—2 Corinthians 3:12, 18

Do you have an outfit that you wear whenever you need to feel
confident and ready to take on the world? Maybe it's just a special
pair of shoes, or a tie, a great hair cut or a favorite song that make
you feel like you could do anything you set your mind to. When you
step out of the house, you feel like a new person. This is what is
evoked when we read this passage. Paul speaks of seeing ourselves
reflecting the glory of the Lord, as Moses did, but without veiling
our faces as Moses did, so that the whole world can see and share in
that glory. He speaks of acting with the same sort of boldness we
have when we put on something that makes us feel great about
ourselves.

Think about when you wear that favorite outfit that gives you
confidence and boldness – not only do you feel like you could do
anything, but people around you pick up that bold spirit as well, and
may take chances just because of your example. Paul does not talk
about putting on the glory of the Lord, as we do an outfit, but in
Romans (13:12, 14) he speaks of putting on the "armor of light" and
even "the Lord Jesus Christ." In Ephesians (4:24, 6:10-17), he talks
about clothing yourself with "the new self created according to the
likeness of God in true righteousness and holiness" and putting on

"the whole armor of God."

There is something about living into this new life in Christ that is like putting on a new outfit. And that outfit will reflect both the holiness of God and be like armor, both of these qualities making us bold and confident as we go out into the world and do as Jesus calls us to do. And we aren't supposed to hide this confidence, this boldness, this glory, but rather let it shine. And by letting it shine, others may be emboldened as well.

Paul has spoken of looking into a mirror in a previous letter to the Corinthians, but in 1 Corinthians 13:12, he speaks of seeing in a mirror only dimly, of a faith that needs to mature, of a future where we will see more clearly. Here it seems as though perhaps the Corinthians are being called to look again into the mirror, and see clearly what God has done in their lives. No longer is it the time for small actions, for dull, unremarkable, average clothing, but time to wear Christ boldly and to be bold. God has given us everything! We should show the whole world! We should be to others as God is to us – loving with abandon, sharing meals with all we meet, telling them about this God who loves us.

Reflect: What makes you feel bold and confident? What if you thought of that as putting on your new self or an armor of light? How would that change how you see the world, and what would you do?

7

Treasure in Clay Jars

2 Corinthians 4:6-15

But we have this treasure in clay jars, so that it may be made clear that this extraordinary power belongs to God and does not come from us. We are afflicted in every way, but not crushed; perplexed, but not driven to despair; persecuted, but not forsaken; struck down, but not destroyed; always carrying in the body the death of Jesus, so that the life of Jesus may also be made visible in our bodies.

—2 Corinthians 4:7-10

Leonard Cohen has a song, *Anthem*, with a great line in the refrain that you may know:

> *There is a crack, a crack in everything*
> *That's how the light gets in.*

Perhaps you've heard this passage from 2 Corinthians 4 quoted, the part about having treasure in clay jars. Maybe you have sung Matt Redman's song, *Trading My Sorrows (Yes, Lord)* that quotes the next few lines of 2 Corinthians. You may not, however, have heard this passage as a whole or remembered that it was all together. There are so many powerful words in just a few, short verses.

When we read the passage as a whole, Paul makes several things clear: Human beings are fragile. Following Jesus Christ will confuse us, hurt us and cause people to make fun of us or even physically harm us. Friends and family might not understand why we do and say the things we believe. And yet, these things will not destroy us. We will stand up again. God is with us all the way. For when we follow in the way of Jesus the Christ, we also carry the life of Christ, and it is our scars, our failures and our cracks, that actually show others the life and light of Jesus.

If we were hermetically sealed, airtight, titanium canisters that wouldn't crack under pressure or break open when banged around, well then we probably wouldn't need the type of healing life Jesus offers. If we had it inside us, no one would be able to see it. It would be hidden away. We are supposed to let that light shine! If we are fragile, clay jars that get chipped and cracked, with pieces shattered or missing, then the light that has taken hold of us and filled us will peek through those imperfections.

Japanese potters have a technique called *Kintsugi*, a means to repair broken pottery that actually transforms it into something new and beautiful. They repair the cracks with lacquer and dust the lacquer with gold so that all of the cracks are now shining with gold. Perhaps that is what Christ does for us – as the love of Christ shines through our broken cracks, those cracks are healed, not so that others cannot see them, but so that they shine with the light of God forever.

If you feel are afflicted in every way, remember you have not been crushed. If at times you feel perplexed, know that you have not been driven to despair. When others persecute you, know that you have not been forsaken. Remember that you have been struck down, but not destroyed. Rejoice when you are persecuted for righteousness' sake. With every blow you are carrying in your body the death of Jesus, so that the life of Jesus may also fill in the cracks.

Reflect: What are some ways that the light of God has shown through your own wounds? How can we be better at becoming vulnerable, allowing others to see our cracks, so they may also see how God has made them beautiful?

8

Things Eternal

2 Corinthians 4:16-5:5

*For we know that if the earthly tent we live in is destroyed,
we have a building from God, a house not made with hands,
eternal in the heavens.*

—2 Corinthians 5:1

The older you get, the more this passage speaks to us. As the years go on, we become more acutely aware of how temporary this earthly tent in which we live is.

It is interesting that Paul uses the metaphor of a tent to speak of things temporary and things eternal. He also speaks of being clothed and never being truly unclothed, even when naked, to further talk about this idea of the things in our lives that can be taken away or destroyed, worn down by old age, and those things that cannot ever be destroyed. Coming on the heels of the treasure stored in clay vessels, we might fall into the easy trap of many Greco-Roman, gnostic, religious ideas of the body as being a frail and inadequate trap for our souls. But rather Paul is not just speaking of the limitations of our human bodies, but of how big God is.

Remember in the days when the Israelites were first wandering in the Sinai wilderness, God called for them to meet in a tent. This was a God who was so overwhelming that you could not meet or see God's face out in the open, otherwise you would face death, so their needed to be some place that mediated the meeting. And yet, this God of ours intended to remain with God's people, not far away, at a mountaintop altar or temple, but in the middle of their lives. So a tent was set up as they camped. A beautiful and detailed tent, festooned with fine embroidery and gold, but a tent nonetheless, something that could easily come down, travel with the people, and be set up yet again. And though the people entered the tent to encounter God, God did not live in the tent. God only visited the tent, when God chose, not just because the people called God's name. Our God cannot be tamed and certainly cannot be contained in even the fanciest tent.

This seems to be Paul's point. The tent is not for God; the tent is for us. We cannot meet God without the tents, the very bodies God made. We cannot meet God without human language, through which we can hear the Word and words of God, and share our experiences of God with one another. Still, these human things, so necessary to our lives, created by God, simply cannot contain God. These human things break, change, and die, but God does not break or die or change. Even though the works we do in God's name might not last forever, God is forever. We can trust in that.

Reflect: In what temporal things have you placed your trust? On what eternal things do you rely? How do you tell the difference?

9

Confidence in God

2 Corinthians 5:1-15

*For the love of Christ urges us on, because we are convinced that
one has died for all; therefore all have died. And he died for all,
so that those who live might live no longer for themselves,
but for him who died and was raised for them.*
—2 Corinthians 5:14-15

A recent New York Times article states that thinking about God
causes people to make bolder choices. A Stanford study showed that
reading about God before making choices involving risk caused
people to more often choose the riskier choice with the greater
payoff. Similarly, in another study by the same scientists, people
were shown advertisements for skydiving, video games and classes
on "how to bribe with little chance of getting caught." For each
product people were shown two different ads, one including the tag
line, "God only knows what you're missing!" Interestingly, all risk is
not the same – with the added tag-line, more people showed interest
in trying sky-diving, whereas there was no increased interest in
learning how to bribe. So, thinking about God can get us to act
boldly, but not thoughtlessly.

With confidence in God, we can take risks for the kingdom: starting
new ministries, volunteering for things that might scare us (like
prison ministries, mission trips to impoverished and/or foreign
places or feeding the homeless), talking to people we don't get along
with, leading worship, being on the music team at church; and so
much else. It is with this confidence that we see elderly people risk
getting arrested for simply feeding hungry people in their cities. It is
also with this confidence that we see people fighting for the rights of

all: marching with protestors of injustice, speaking up for immigrants, standing by the side of young women seeking abortions just to make sure they are safe.

What wild dream do you have? What dreams do you have for your church, your life in faith or the Church universal? We can get the confidence to take risks to follow those dreams (and sometimes fail spectacularly) by keeping God in our lives and minds – by reading scripture, praying, being part of a church community. It seems so simple, and yet even science says confidence in God can free us.

Reflect: Where do you need confidence? What is the wildest dream you have for your life? For your family? For your church? Write them down, stick them somewhere readily visible, and pray about them today, and each time you see them.

10

Reconciliation

Corinthians 5:16-6:1

So if anyone is in Christ, there is a new creation: everything old has passed away; see, everything has become new! All this is from God, who reconciled us to himself through Christ, and has given us the ministry of reconciliation...

—2 Corinthians 5:17-18

Reconciliation is one of the toughest things Jesus asks us to do. It is hard to forget all of the hurt people have caused us, even when we are ready to forgive them, and move forward. Reconciliation requires more work than simply saying the words, "I was wrong and I'm sorry," and "I forgive you." It requires vigilance, and to truly see one another as a new creation, not as the same old people we were before. And it means that we have to keep ourselves from falling into old patterns – of quickly snapping at someone who has hurt us, but who is trying to be different. We have to let people be new.

How many times in an argument with a loved one does all the stuff you both did in the past come up? This is the sort of obstacle we have to avoid when we want to live into new lives. Because if you forgive someone, but then hold onto the old junk that happened, you are the one mired in that old life – you can't see the other person in a new light, and you are also not living a new life. It's repeating the past, which is like eating leftover meatloaf from last week – it tastes bad and will probably make you sick.

This is not to say that everything old is bad. Fine wines are often best when aged. But we cannot live on fine wines alone. The Hebrew and Greek scriptures are life-giving, but only when we can understand them in our own words, and apply them in our lives today. Holding onto old hurts and grudges is not life-giving. In fact, holding on to grudges turns you into the person you are condemning, someone who hurts others out of your own pain.

We need to choose new life instead. Like a garden needs to be weeded regularly, our hearts and minds need to be tended, pulling out the weeds of petty arguments and sharp words, so that love, kindness and trust can grow. So if you are living out reconciliation with another person or a group of people, try to see them through the eyes of love first. You will see whether or not they have been transformed through God's grace and forgiveness. If they continue to behave in the old, hurtful ways, you can still be reconciled to them by keeping your heart kind and peaceful – hoping the best for them, but simply choosing not to engage them anymore. This stuff is not easy. Jesus never said it would be. It is the hardest thing in the world. And it is the most rewarding.

Reflect: Do you tend to hold grudges? Do you forgive easily? What does it, or would it, look like to forgive every person who hurts you, and keep working at it?

11

An Acceptable Time

2 Corinthians 6:1-13

As we work together with him, we urge you also not to accept the grace of God in vain. For he says,
  "At an acceptable time I have listened to you,
    and on a day of salvation I have helped you."

See, now is the acceptable time; see, now is the day of salvation!

— 2 Corinthians 6:1-2

P aul is encouraging the Corinthians to be who they are created to be, loving and generous. We can tell that Paul saw these qualities in the Corinthians when he visited them, and also sees these qualities in their actions to forgive and reinstate the member who had so egregiously hurt the community. He does not want them to stop at this action, but keep spreading their love and generosity beyond the body, right there, right then. They did not need to wait for Paul's next visit or any new sign of the Holy Spirit. The day of salvation was already there, so the acceptable time for action was upon them.

Paul quotes Isaiah because Isaiah was speaking to a people facing an invading army. They didn't have time to wait for another savior. God had already given them everything they needed to be saved. They just needed to be the faithful people God had called them to be all along:

Thus says the LORD:
In a time of favor I have answered you,
on a day of salvation I have helped you;
I have kept you and given you

as a covenant to the people,
to establish the land,
to apportion the desolate heritages;

—Isaiah 49:8

Like the Judeans, the Corinthians already had everything they needed. They already had kind and generous spirits. They had Christ's words through Paul. They knew how to forgive well. They had privilege and resources other churches didn't even have. There was nothing to stop them from living out the life Christ desired for them, and doing it well.

Paul lists his own faithful actions, not as a boast about his faithfulness, but as examples of things the Corinthians were also fully capable of doing as faithful servants of God. It is a concrete list of things they might do or face, beyond forgiveness, faithfulness, becoming humble, and giving generously. Paul shows the wide range of faithful acts one might do in service of Christ: "through great endurance, in afflictions, hardships, calamities, beatings, imprisonments, riots, labors, sleepless nights, hunger; by purity, knowledge, patience, kindness, holiness of spirit, genuine love, truthful speech…" (2 Corinthians 6:5-7a). Many of these things the Corinthians have witnessed in Paul already, and none of them are beyond the abilities of their community to do as well.

Paul uses the Isaiah quote as encouragement – the Judeans were able to remain safe and hold onto Jerusalem because of their faithful and immediate action.

The day of salvation has not passed, today is an acceptable time. The day of reconciliation has not passed. Don't wait another minute. Don't let God's grace be in vain. Enjoy the benefits of God's grace now. Act boldly and faithfully to love the world today.

Reflect: Have you felt a call on your heart and mind to do something bold in the name of God? What is stopping you from acting on that call right now?

12

They Shall Be My People

2 Corinthians 6:14-7:1

What agreement has the temple of God with idols? For we
are the temple of the living God; as God said,
"I will live in them and walk among them,
and I will be their God,
and they shall be my people.

—2 Corinthians 6:16

This section of 2 Corinthians, from 6:14-7:1, makes an abrupt change in tone, language and subject-matter from the verses that directly surround it – 6:13 and 7:2 both refer to Paul's request that the Corinthians open their hearts to him. This is clearly a digression, marked with rhetorical questions. What does God have to do with idols?

Throughout this letter, Paul expresses his love for the Corinthians. He also shares his concern about them possibly following charismatic, but misleading teachers. There seems to be a rift between Paul and the Corinthians because of a a troubling situation and a distressing letter, which we do not have, and that fact that he has not been able to visit in a while (see June 6 reflection). He seems eager to repair this rift and also to encourage the Corinthians to not lose heart in him or his teachings, even though he is not present. He wants to warn them against spending too much time with, or giving too much credence to, teachings that are idolatrous or fanciful versions of Christianity.

Many will recognize the beginning of verse 6:14 – "Do not be mismatched with unbelievers." Many of us will have heard this quoted, or said it ourselves in reference to marriages between Christians and non-Christians. This interpretation, however, is unlikely, since the text never talk about married persons. In other letters, including 1 Corinthians, Paul does not seem to have a problem with believers being married to unbelievers, in fact encouraging such marriages to remain intact, in the hopes that the unbeliever might eventually be drawn into the Christian community of his or her spouse. Likewise, Paul does not seem to desire Christians to abandon friendships or business partnerships with non-Christians, but rather understands both the necessity of remaining in the world, and in relationship with non-Christians, both for pragmatic reasons as well as the possibilities of drawing them into the Christian community.

So what is Paul talking about? Apparently some Corinthians have failed to grasp the implications of being in Christ. If the Corinthians believe in the hope and grace of God, if they are "temples of the living God" in the world, then they should not be participating in the cultic rites of the pagan temples. The Corinthian Christians were to love all people, but not become involved with the pagan cult.

Paul is not warning us to stay away from people who are not Christians, but rather to stay away from pagan practices and superstitions that lead us away from Christ. It is one thing to love someone who is not Christian. It is entirely another to be drawn into ways of life that involve us in theft, dishonesty, drunkenness, sexual immorality. Perhaps the test is this: Who is having the greatest effect on whom? If developing relationships with those far from Christ brings them in, then all is well. If it draws us more towards an unhealthy lifestyle, then perhaps we are not in a good place to be a witness in that circumstance. Paul offers a wise caution.

Reflect: When did a relationship drag you into a bad place? When have you been able to bring someone else into a better place? How might you tell the difference?

13

Weathering the Storms of Conflict

2 Corinthians 7:2-16

For even when we came into Macedonia, our bodies had no rest, but we were afflicted in every way—disputes without and fears within. But God, who consoles the downcast, consoled us by the arrival of Titus, and not only by his coming, but also by the consolation with which he was consoled about you, as he told us of your longing, your mourning, your zeal for me, so that I rejoiced still more.

—2 Corinthians 7:5-7

As we have seen, Paul seems extraordinarily concerned about the brokenness in his relationship with the Corinthians, and here we see that he is relieved to have heard from Titus that the rift is being mended. Paul returns to the hurt caused by the individual within the church community at Corinth that caused pain within the community, and also between themselves and Paul because of a previous letter he wrote advising them on what they should do. We can see how sin does not simply affect those directly involved, but ripples out to cause hurt in a larger group.

We have all seen this happen – when someone has caused hurt there are many reactions among the witnesses. Some people will leap to defend the offender, some will rush to condemn, and some will just desire peace, regardless of the offender's guilt or innocence. Even within these three major groups, there will be splinters – people who believe the person is innocent, no matter the facts; people who believe in the offender's innocence until facts are laid out; people who believe the offender guilty, but believe another chance should be given; and those people who are defending the accused offender. Sin causes division and mistrust that is difficult to overcome.

Paul thinks he might have overestimated the good faith between himself and the Corinthians in writing a stern letter encouraging them to deal with the offender without leniency. And likely the letter did cause people to get mad at Paul, and some probably even left the community over it. It is rare to see a conflict in the church that gets resolved without someone leaving. Ultimately, it is the faith in Christ, and Paul's teachings about Jesus and the way Jesus loves that causes the Corinthians to come together again, heal their division, and compel the offending party to repent and reconcile with the community.

Paul hears of this from Titus, who he has rushed to meet in Macedonia, hoping for this very news. He is relieved both that the Corinthians were able to see through their anger and division to trust in his tough words to them, and that they were able to initiate healing because of those words. He had been boasting of their faith and generosity on his travels to other churches, and this conflict had distracted them from doing the central work of Christ.

Of course, it is this way with all new groups. In 1965 educational psychologist Bruce Tuckman proposed a 4-stage process that happens with groups gathered around a particular purpose: Forming, Storming, Norming and Performing. The Corinthians were going to have a storm in the life of their group. The question was whether or not they could weather it. Faith in Jesus Christ, a faith founded on resurrection and forgiveness, is ideal for weathering the storms of life. Paul knew this, and the Corinthians were able to see their faith in action by putting it to the test. When love is strong, we can weather the inevitable storms of conflict.

Reflect: Think about a group conflict in which you have been a part. Was it simply part of the growing pains of a group, or was it destructive? Was the conflict handled well? If it had been understood whether the conflict was constructive or destructive, do you think it would have been handled differently?

14

Generosity in Affliction

2 Corinthians 8:1-7

...for during a severe ordeal of affliction,
their abundant joy and their extreme poverty
have overflowed in a wealth of generosity on their part.

—2 Corinthians 8:2

There is a typical scene you might see on a playground: a group of boys is playing soccer. They obviously only need one ball for this, but there are a pile of balls on the side, stock-piled. Some girls on the playground want to use a ball for their game, but the boys keep telling them they need *all* of the balls, "just in case," and the girls are confused and mad at this ridiculous hoarding. This is also like the behavior we saw in so many large, rich companies in the recent past that held onto the extra profits they were making after our most recent recession began to turn around. Our government invested our money in many ways in order to stimulate the economy, intending that when the economy improved, such companies could hire more people or buy more raw resources to make more products, not so they could hoard resources for a rainy day, which was not doing anyone any good.

The Bible has a lot to say about how we use our money. Jesus told the parable of the rich man whose land was so abundant he had to build bigger barns, but it was clear that this man was hoarding his grain much like the large companies are hoarding profits, only for themselves. In Genesis, Joseph interprets the Pharaoh's dreams of an upcoming famine, and urges the Pharaoh to store up the current abundance of crops to prepare for the famine, which is done, not for the Pharaoh's household alone, but for the whole land. This action saves Egypt and many other lands because it was not done out of selfishness.

Paul holds up the generosity of the Macedonians not because they had an abundance to share, but because they joyfully offered up everything they could in service to God, despite having very little. The Corinthians had everything. Holding onto it just in case they began to experience similar persecution would not grow the church. Holding onto it would only help themselves, and only in the short term.

Holding onto what we have been given instead of offering it back for God's use elsewhere kills our souls, our faith and our communities. Then there would be nothing worth holding onto. By giving generously there might be other disciples gathered into the body to support each other in hard times.

Too often we think we will not have enough for ourselves in an emergency if we give too much away. And yet, time and again the feeding of the 5,000 becomes a reality. We don't know how it works, we just know that it does. When we share what we have in the midst of scarcity, everyone has more than enough of what they need. Our God is a God of abundance, not a God of scarcity.

Reflect: Think of a time that you thought there would not be enough to go around, but when everyone shared what they had to offer, there was more than enough for everyone. How might we remind ourselves to keep believing in a God of abundance rather than a God of scarcity?

15

Genuine Love

2 Corinthians 8:7-15

Now as you excel in everything—in faith, in speech, in knowledge, in utmost eagerness, and in our love for you—so we want you to excel also in this generous undertaking. I do not say this as a command, but I am testing the genuineness of your love against the earnestness of others.

—2 Corinthians 8:7-8

Paul is proud of the Corinthians. He has boasted of their faith and understanding of Jesus' teachings, of their generosity and eagerness to give more, to serve more. They have also weathered a storm within their community through their love for one another and are stronger for it. Now it is time to take that love and spread it further. If the Corinthians only have love for one another, it is not really following the will of Jesus to go and make disciples of all nations. To only show love to one another would be hiding their light under a bushel basket, and that light of love was given to them to share with others. Now that they have resolved their internal conflict, it is time to show how that love and faith can heal other wounds in the world.

Paul wants the Corinthians to get out in the world and show love to others in their community, but he and the other apostles have also promised to take up a collection of funds for the church in Jerusalem, which is suffering from persecution. As we have seen in this and most of Paul's other letters, the work they are doing as apostles could not have succeeded without monetary support from individuals and churches. They recognize their indebtedness to the church in Jerusalem, the very beginning of this dangerous ministry of love. Sometimes we think that the Holy Spirit will simply provide financial resources for ministry, like manna from heaven, and forget that we are part of God's plan for the Spirit's work in the world.

Prayer is meaningless without change in our own actions, just as Paul has already said in 1 Corinthians 13, "If I speak in the tongues of mortals and of angels, but do not have love, I am a noisy gong or a clanging cymbal." Love is a concrete thing. When we say, "I'll pray for you," do we follow it up with acts of love, or do we immediately forget about what we prayed for, moving on with our everyday lives? Paul is asking the Corinthians to make their genuine love concrete – in their actions toward one another, toward those outside the community, and in support of other churches, both spiritually and financially.

It is all well and good for Paul to speak highly of the Corinthians' generosity and faithfulness, but if they do not act in generous and faithful ways, it simply isn't true. In this case, part of the church was asking for support in a trying time, and Paul was encouraging the churches he knew intimately to contribute to a love offering. These churches knew Paul to be a true and faithful teacher, so there was no reason not to follow through.

Love is such an overused word. How can we begin to use it only when we mean it? What does love even mean to us? Jesus talked about what it looks like to love others. Perhaps if we measure our daily actions against those concrete, earthy commandments, we will better be able to see if and what we truly love.

Reflect: Do you have any generous undertakings? Have you planned your giving for this year? If you line up the things you say are important in life, and your checkbook ledger, do they line up?

16

Eagerness in Service

2 Corinthians 8:16-24

And with them we are sending our brother whom we have often tested and found eager in many matters, but who is now more eager than ever because of his great confidence in you.

—2 Corinthians 8:22

Do you have any worker bees in your church or workplace who you know will show up to help whenever needed? Workers who neither take over a project, nor expect special recognition, nor get overwhelmed or burned out, but can be relied on for busy hands, warm hearts and encouraging words?

This seems to be the type of person Titus was. Whenever Paul speaks of him in 2 Corinthians, it is of Titus' tireless hard work, faithfulness and eagerness in service. Paul has complete faith in sending Titus to Corinth when he realizes he will not be able to get there as quickly as he (and the Corinthians) had hoped. His faith is not misplaced. Titus seems to have reassured the Corinthians as they worried Paul had abandoned them, and also bears witness to the difficult but successful reintegration of the member who had done harm within the community.

Workers such as Titus are a gift to the church. They not only get plenty done, especially the tasks that are tedious or get overlooked, but they are wonderful examples of how to be servant leaders. It is rare to see someone jump in eagerly to take on the tasks of a community with no complaint and no requirement of recognition.

This refreshing and infectious. Knowing that someone like Titus will definitely be at the next highway cleanup or helping with Vacation Bible School makes others want to join in and help, too. You know that the work will be made easy and fun with people who are cheerful and eager to work hard.

Titus was not simply Paul's proxy, a pale substitute for his mentor. He had wonderful gifts to share that helped keep communities together and growing. We don't know everything Titus did or said, but it is clear that his time with the Corinthians helped them get through the aftermath of a difficult conflict, and to keep enjoying one another. Because of Titus' presence, they were ready to move forward in eager service in their community and beyond, following Titus' lead.

The good news is that it's never too late to become a Titus in your life. Who out there is doing God's work, in need of your help? Does the worship committee need help setting up? Do they need help with the games at VBS? You were a kid once, right? Are volunteers needed to stay overnight in order to host homeless families at church?

Can you name the Tituses in your congregation? Maybe you are one of them yourself. What can you do to be eager in service, and encourage others to do the same?

17

Cheerful Giving

2 Corinthians 9:1-7

The point is this: the one who sows sparingly will also reap sparingly, and the one who sows bountifully will also reap bountifully. Each of you must give as you have made up your mind, not reluctantly or under compulsion, for God loves a cheerful giver.

—2 Corinthians 9:6-7

One of the strangest things that many churches do is to quote 2 Corinthians 9:7 – "Each of you must give as you have made up your mind, not reluctantly or under compulsion, for God loves a cheerful giver" – as we go into the offering during Sunday services. The words we say suggest we want you to give freely and cheerfully, and simply respond to God's gifts of love and grace, but by saying it out loud, it often sounds like we are saying, "Give FREELY and CHEERFULLY. You know how God *loves* a CHEERFUL GIVER." Sometimes the good intentions we have to encourage giving make us less cheerful givers and more suspicious givers.

But we really do want to give. God has given us so much, and, on our best days, most are generous people who can't give enough away. We want to share all the love and resources we have received. We want others to know how much they are loved, and if someone is in need we want to share what we have. We all need a little help from time to time. How can we be people who are open and loving and generous all the time? How can we be cheerful givers who are easy to approach when someone does need help, like Paul is hoping the Corinthians will be when the Macedonians come to collect an offering to support a poorer church?

If you give out of guilt, or under pressure, then the gift is given, but the heart remains unchanged. If we pressure people into giving, we may get the gift, but find them filled with resentment. What we really want is to encourage lavish, uncompelled, voluntary generosity.

A woman once asked for a ride from her neighbor. It wasn't a huge favor, just a few miles away, and her neighbor was always happy to help others, but the woman had a hard time asking. They didn't know each other very well. They had said, "Hi," a few times, and occasionally their daughters played together, but they didn't know much about each other. As they drove, the women began to chat. The woman who had asked for a ride admitted she had been reluctant to ask for help for a couple of reasons. One reason was that she wasn't sure if her neighbor would readily agree to help her. The neighbor was a bit reserved, and the woman wasn't sure if that was because the neighbor was shy or unfriendly. The neighbor was chagrined. She didn't mean to come across in an unfriendly manner, but she did take a while to warm up to new people, though, she was always happy to help others. As they continued to talk, she thought about how she might act differently so people knew she was open to friendship and to offering a helping hand.

The other reason the woman had been reluctant to ask for help is why most of us are reluctant to ask for help; we think we need to take care of all of our needs out of our own resources. The woman admitted that she had a hard time asking for help, but that recently God seemed to be sending a lot of signs that she needed to be better about letting others help her. The neighbor chuckled and said that she often received similar signs from God. The first woman had great courage in asking for help from her neighbor. It was lucky her neighbor was friendlier than she first appeared. In fact, her neighbor was quite a cheerful giver. Perhaps, if she had been warmer, the woman might not have been so worried to ask for even a little favor.

To be cheerful givers, we need to be cheerful. We don't have to be happy every moment of our lives, and we don't need to pretend to be cheerful when we are not.

Sometimes we worry that our gifts will not be used wisely, but when we remember how much we love to share what God has given us, doesn't that make us delighted? We might even give a smile as we put our offering in the plate. When we give cheerfully, we might get asked to help some more. Then, as we give, that cheer will grow. We will grow, and then keep on giving.

Reflect: Would people describe you as a cheerful giver? How can we stop being afraid to ask for help, or to offer help to others without worrying whether that help will be squandered?

18

God's Providence

2 Corinthians 9:8-15

He who supplies seed to the sower and bread for food will supply and multiply your seed for sowing and increase the harvest of your righteousness. ...for the rendering of this ministry not only supplies the needs of the saints but also overflows with many thanksgivings to God.

—2 Corinthians 9:10, 12

There is a wonderful story of generosity that happened in a small church, in a small, rural community without a lot of economic growth or opportunities. They had been gifted for almost 30 years by having a part-time pastor whose real income came from his law practice. In all that time, he hadn't accepted a raise, knowing the finances were slim, and wanting to dedicate as much money as possible into the mission of the church beyond his salary. Sometime in the 1990's the church had been left shares in an oil well, which was helpful, but unreliable. One of the difficult conversations they needed to have was that if they wanted to continue as a congregation, they might need to make an investment in a full-time pastor's salary, trusting that the investment would pay off in the future.

It was a sensitive topic, but a conversation that became much easier after a particular encounter with the generosity of the Holy Spirit in action. The church had long supported a boarding school for impoverished and orphaned boys in southeast Oklahoma, started and run by the denomination. They gave regular monthly contributions, and one of the members was even on the board of the school. One month he approached the church leadership with a request that they give the school an additional one-time gift of $10,000 to cover a shortfall they were experiencing in a tough economic time when giving was down. Though the economy was suffering in general, oil prices were high, and the church had received a large stipend from the oil shares left to them, enough to cover such a gift and still pay all of their other expenses. Trusting in their mission to follow Jesus Christ, and to give what they could to those who were in need, they made the gift.

That faithfulness and generosity of this tiny congregation was incredible, but even more incredible was when the treasurer reported the very next month they had received almost exactly $10,000 in revenue from their oil shares, replacing what the church had given away. It brings to mind Ecclesiastes 11:1 – "Send out your bread upon the waters, for after many days you will get it back." After that conversations about finances and the future became easier, even joyful. In trusting that God would continue to give abundantly, the church was able to live more fully.

It doesn't always work out that neatly. There are times we give sacrificially and still struggle, but rarely do people give generously and regret it. The rewards for lavish generosity are out of this world.

The Holy Spirit worked many small miracles in that congregation, but this was a big one. God has already given abundantly. Can we not trust that God will continue to do the same? This is truly a leap of faith.

Reflect: Is there something you feel called to do but are worried that any time, energy or money invested will be wasted? What would your leap of faith look like?

19

You Belong to Christ

2 Corinthians 10:1-7

If you are confident that you belong to Christ, remind yourself of this, that just as you belong to Christ, so also do we.

—2 Corinthians 10:7

In chapter 10, Paul seems to be especially concerned that we do not compare ourselves to others, whether positively or negatively. Here he warns against putting ourselves above others simply because we are Christians. We do not become angels or perfect when we are baptized. We do not shed our bodies, even though our bodies can get injured and perish. God values our earthy creation. After all, God made us. These bodies are fragile. They share a commonality with the animal, plants, dirt and even the stars because God has woven us into creation intentionally.

We are called to care for creation, not escape it. God's vision for heaven on earth is not that everything will be replaced by better, more durable stuff, but that the fragile bodies we have will exhibit eternal love and life even through the cycles of living and dying. When we are "in Christ" we do not shed the things that make us human, but we embrace them. We see our bodies as beautiful and useful to God. Even our weaknesses can be used for God's work and glory.

Therefore, we do not judge our failings and the failings of others. If we try something and simply fail, it is not necessarily a sin. We need to see that not all failures separate us from God. In fact, our failures are often where God works most powerfully. What separates us from

God is hurting one another and God's creation, yet even that can be overcome by God's love and forgiveness.

So when people are not perfect in how they try to do God's will, we remember that we, too, are not perfectly obedient, either. We believe in Christ, tryuing to follow Christ, but we still fail and lose our way sometimes. Paul reminds us that we do not become perfect simply because we are Christians, rather it is how we deal with our failings and imperfections that is different, and not human. Through God's love and gifts of grace, we can be restored, made whole. We can offer the same to others, handling arguments with love, not judging others for their failures, but seeing them as children of God. We can help others see that they are loved even when they fail, and hopefully as our community will surround us with love when we fail.

What does a world without God's love offer a human being? Only death. We have been offered so much more, and when we say we love and believe in Jesus the Christ, we need to show that love to other people, not judgment. We are not better than anyone else because we are Christian – we hurt and get hurt, we live, we die – but we have been given the gift of a life that is connected to all of God's creation, and so our failings don't have to define us. They can be overcome.

Have you ever judged someone else for a mistake, then found yourself making the same mistake? How did that feel? What might someone say to you, to would help you move on from that mistake, and feel loved?

20

Bragging Rights

2 Corinthians 10:8-18

We do not dare to classify or compare ourselves with some of those who commend themselves. But when they measure themselves by one another, and compare themselves with one another, they do not show good sense. We, however, will not boast beyond limits, but will keep within the field that God has assigned to us, to reach out even as far as you.

—2 Corinthians 10:12-13

Paul is upset that some "false teachers" have entered his mission field. They are measuring themselves by one another, rather by a greater standard by which things should be measured.

Paul was the first to bring the gospel of Jesus Christ to the people of Corinth. He does not want to go beyond his bounds, by meddling in others' work, but neither does he want someone meddling in his mission field.

It's not a matter of boasting for Paul. It's a matter of staying in bounds. If you stay in bounds, you earn some bragging rights. In the end, Paul says in the last verse of chapter 10, it really doesn't matter how much people commend themselves. What really matters is whom the Lord commends.

We can brag on ourselves, but that will only puff us up. What really matters is what God thinks. Time will bear this out. Paul is proud of what God has done in Corinth through his ministry. He doesn't want to pretend otherwise.

There is some tension between Jesus instructing his followers in the

Sermon on the Mount not to sound a trumpet before them as the hypocrites do, and in the same sermon to say, "Let your light so shine before others so that they see your good works and glorify your Father in heaven." Which is it? Are we to humbly not boast of our good works, or are we to let our light shine? How might we know the difference?

Perhaps it comes down to motive. Are you boasting to gain glory for yourself, or for God? When you boast, will people talk about how wonderful you are, or how wonderful God is?

For Paul, boasting about what God is doing, is not a problem. Boasting about his weakness is not a problem. On the other hand, if one reads enough of Paul's letters, one often wonders if boasting might have been one of Paul's problems, perhaps even his "thorn in the flesh."

Reflect: By what standard do you measure yourself? What do you consider your field? About what do you tend to boast the most?

21

All That Glitters is Not Gold

2 Corinthians 11:1-15

I may be untrained in speech, but not in knowledge; certainly in
every way and in all things we have made this evident to you...
As the truth of Christ is in me, this boast of mine will not be silenced
in the regions of Achaia.

—2 Corinthians 11:6, 10

There is an episode of the television version of 'Little House on the Prairie' where Laura and a friend, Jonah, discover what looks like gold ore in the stream where they are fishing. They pan it, dream big dreams, and can't wait to share their newfound fortune with their families. The "gold" turns out to be fool's gold (pyrite). Laura is crushed, sad and humiliated, when telling Pa about it. Pa reminds her that he and Ma do not love her and her sisters for what fortunes they might bring home, but rather for who they are. Similarly, Paul tells the Corinthians that the teachers and apostles coming to them with the biggest boasts about themselves and their teaching are not worth as much as they appear, whereas Paul, who seems like a fool, or fool's gold, is the real thing.

Paul can boast of the only thing worth boasting about, not his own life or works, but of Jesus Christ's life and work. He also notes that he boasts of the church in Corinth, even saying he "robbed" other churches by accepting their support while working with the Corinthians. In light of other parts of this letter, it is hard to imagine Paul really believes he was using the support of the other churches foolishly, but rather since he is speaking of boasting here, he exaggerates his language to match his claims. Foolish boasting is a familiar rhetorical device in Paul's day.

Paul is often taken for a fool, traveling all over starting new communities in the name of a God who died for humanity's sins. What could be sillier than that? In order to do that well, Paul must humble himself, often be humiliated, and compete with teachers with grand claims of the powers of their beliefs and gods. He is willing to name the criticisms that might be leveled at him, such as wasting the money of the churches supporting him.

It is a difficult thing to cut through grand claims and slick marketing to see if the heart of something is true or fool's gold. Paul shows us that he is not trying to cover the truth of Christianity with pretty lies, or the truth about his own hardships. He lays it bare that following Christ might cause you to look like a fool. People will accuse you of calling attention to yourself, of wasting your time and their money. Heck, you might even be imprisoned, beaten or killed for living out God's truth and teachings.

Anyone telling you anything else should be viewed with suspicion. For, as the old spiritual says, Jesus is enough for us. Paul doesn't worry about looking like a fool. He doesn't care about much other than living into his own salvation. It is about spreading the love and truth of God in Christ. It is the only way to find life. All other teaching is simply fool's gold.

Reflect: When have you been hoodwinked by a cheap fake? Are there versions of Christianity that seem like fool's gold? How might you identify the real thing?

22

Foolish Love

2 Corinthians 11:16-12:1

Who is weak, and I am not weak?
Who is made to stumble, and I am not indignant?
If I must boast, I will boast of the things that show my weakness.

—2 Corinthians 12:11-21

We have already seen that Paul is unconcerned about looking foolish (and also about boasting). He worries about relationships being strained between him and beloved churches. Paul hopes people don't think he is wasting their support. He prays for conflict within churches to be resolved, but he does not worry about looking like a fool. He knows that the foolish love of God will bring life to us, a people who keep doing things that only lead to death.

Paul may not be worried about looking like a fool, but we certainly do. We even cringe when others are embarrassing themselves, as if it were being reflected onto us just because we're in the same room. One of the areas we can see this most prevalently is in trying to get people unused to public speaking and performing to use big actions and project their words. We often think if we are quiet and don't move around a lot, we will simply blend into the background, and people in the audience won't notice us. This may work in everyday life, but on stage, the bigger the better. In fact, you will draw more attention to yourself and look silly when you are in front of an audience if you don't get into singing and speaking boldly with large actions that can be seen and understood by everyone. For one thing, if you are relaxed and having fun, so will they. But also, you're trying to draw people into the action, the mood, and the subject you are portraying.

The same principles of good stagecraft apply in our lives of faith. Paul was trying to show people what life in Christ was like. He needed to be bold, and live out God's command to love with big gestures. We probably wouldn't know anything about Paul if he had gone into towns, spoken quietly and gently, and complied with polite society manners.

Paul may have seemed foolish, but people also thought Jesus was a fool to eat with prostitutes and tax collectors, to love people who didn't have any money or power, to heal the homeless and jobless – what did these people contribute to society? And then Jesus even died for them. The most foolish act of all. Paul knew there was no bold act, no foolish deed of love that could compare to that, but he sought to love as foolishly as Jesus.

To do anything great, we need to be willing to risk looking foolish. It's quite funny to watch the various attempts of flight. Some were disastrous. Others were hilarious.

We try to hide our weakness, our foolishness. It is, however, most often how God acts in the world. Our weakness reveals our humanity. It bonds us with others. It allows people to identify with us.

Reflect? What is something foolish you can do that would show someone that they are loved no matter what? What weaknesses do you hide that might be ways God will use you to bless others?

23

Pride Goeth Before the Fall

2 Corinthians 12:1-21

Therefore, to keep me from being too elated, a thorn was given me in the flesh, a messenger of Satan to torment me, to keep me from being too elated. Three times I appealed to the Lord about this, that it would leave me, ⁹but he said to me, "My grace is sufficient for you, for power is made perfect in weakness."

So, I will boast all the more gladly of my weaknesses, so that the power of Christ may dwell in me.

—2 Corinthians 12:7-9

Paul is rounding the bend for the final stretch, and so are we. Here Paul puts forth his final arguments. He begins by describing a mystical, perhaps out-of-body experience that he had 14 years ago. He was taken up into the third heaven. Jewish writers of that day often debated how many levels of heaven there were. Paul calls this level, "Paradise." There he saw amazing things. If his opponents have had visions, he wants the Corinthians to know he has too.

We often forget that Paul is a mystic. He converted from persecuting Christians to becoming one, because of a personal revelation, in which Jesus Christ struck him blind and said, "Why are you persecuting me?" He became the greatest missionary for those he previously persecuted.

Even with all his visions and revelations, Paul has a problem of some sort. It could be a physical problem. (He says the Galatian church was so loving they would have given him their eyes if they could.) Might Paul's problem be a vision problem? Keep in mind that scales fell from his eyes after his conversion. On the other hand, maybe his problem is a sin that he can't overcome. He never says, and we'll never know, but Paul believes he has this problem to keep him humble. His missionary efforts have been incredibly successful. He has planted Christianity across the Roman Empire, even into Europe. He could get a big head, but this thorn in the flesh, whatever it is, keeps him humble.

Paul is not powerful. He is not a big person. In fact, the word "Paul" means "small." He has been beaten nearly to death, shipwrecked and imprisoned. He is probably feeble. This is why he can say, "Though our outward nature is wasting away, our inward nature is being renewed daily." The power of his proclamation came not from his physical prowess, but from his humility and weakness.

So it is with the church. When we insist on our own way or boast of our great strength, we miss our calling. It is through our kindness, our humility, our gentleness and willingness to listen that we will find our voice, and experience the power of the gospel.

Jesus wears a crown of thorns. His power comes through weakness. Paul has a thorn in the flesh. His power comes through weakness.

Reflect: Proverbs 16:18 says, "Pride goes before the fall." When has this been true for you? In what ways have you found grace and joy in weakness or humility?

24

Accountability

2 Corinthians 13:1-7

Examine yourselves to see whether you are living in the faith. Test yourselves. Do you not realize that Jesus Christ is in you?— unless, indeed, you fail to meet the test!

—2 Corinthians 13:5

In this letter, Paul has been anxious that the Corinthians see him as a faithful friend rather than as a disinterested stranger. We have talked about his love for the Corinthians, which he wants them to see despite their separation in distance and time. He also is concerned that the community he helped form will continue intact, and follow Jesus in the ways they need to, rather than simply in name only. But Paul also has some difficult things to tell at least some of the members of their community, and he wants to make sure they know he is doing it out of love. He warns them that he will not be lenient or tolerant of behavior that does not match followers of Christ.

Though Paul can be quite parental at times, he most often refers to himself as "brother" or "friend" in his letters. When he calls others to task for their sinfulness, he does so as another member of the body, not as the head of the body. He calls for them first to test themselves to see whether they are indeed living out the faith they proclaim.

The sort of accountability Paul exhibits here and elsewhere in his letters is that of Matthew 18, where Jesus instructs his followers how to deal with conflict in the community. He instructs them first to speak with that person in private, then to bring two or three witnesses if the other person's offense continues after the first conversation, and then before the whole community. If those things don't work, sometimes we must go our separate ways.

Immediately following this, Jesus tells Peter that if someone sins against him, he is to forgive not simply seven times, but rather seventy-seven times. So, there are consequences to continued sin. Like a cancer in the body, one cannot continue to harm the community and expect to remain a part of it. Yet, there is also forgiveness. Those who sin against one another cannot be part of the body any longer, but the members are still to show love and forgiveness even as they are set apart.

We see Jesus' words echoed here in Paul's talk of witnesses, and of not being too lenient, for, if you love someone, how can you let them continue to harm others and, thereby, themselves? Sometimes those conversations are difficult. Sometimes they require witnesses. They may even require a relationship with the community to end. If we do this without love, there is no hope for possible restoration. In order to hold people accountable, we need to have a relationship built on trust and love. There is little hope for change if the people we hold accountable think we do not actually care about them and want to help them.

If we make mistakes, we want someone who cares about us to talk to us about them. It is easier to face difficult change if someone is pointing it out to us in love, not trying to humiliate us. To be faithful members of this body of Christ, we are called to love and to hold each other accountable to the way of righteousness, even if that means some hard conversations.

Reflect: In your life, who holds you accountable? Who can call you out if you are off base? When has God called you to hold others accountable?

25

Putting Things in Order

2 Corinthians 13:8-13

Finally, brothers and sisters, farewell. Put things in order, listen to my appeal, agree with one another, live in peace; and the God of love and peace will be with you.

—2 Corinthians 13:11

Put things in order. Such a simple, firm, but loving, command from Paul. It is a command that echoes down the millennia to us today. The Corinthians led busy, complicated lives. Business, friends and shiny new ideas competed with the teachings of the love and life that conquers death of Jesus Christ. Does that sound familiar? It is the chaos and messiness of life that we recognize from our everyday lives.

Put things in order. How quickly chaos creeps in. No matter how clean the house, a few days of mail unattended, or not putting things back after we're finished with them, and it seems as bad as it ever was. And the dust! Oh the dust! Even if you dust every day, it seems to settle right back where it was - a never-ending, thankless task.

So it goes with our relationships, too. If we do not tend to them consistently, in a timely manner, things can get messy quickly, through miscommunication, misunderstanding and mistakes, all becoming like so many piles of paper on the kitchen counter. When we put aside seemingly little things, like simply saying, "Good morning," or, "How are you?" (and meaning it), we lose touch with one another. We don't know all the little things going on in each other's worlds.

Paul calls the Corinthians to pull the weeds, to put things in order. Simple words for something that does not seem so simple.

Fortunately, Paul does not leave us without a way to get there. He offers us the reconciling love of Christ, which transcends all things. He encourages us to open our hearts. He says – listen to me, agree with one another and live in peace. Keep listening to what is true. Find ways to agree with those who profess Christ along with you. Don't start fights with them or those outside the body of Christ. Don't complicate things, or assume what others are thinking or feeling. If you have questions, ask them. Be okay with not always agreeing with others so long as it doesn't prevent the kingdom of God from growing.

Paul's Second Letter to the Corinthians is an appeal to an open heart. We, and the Corinthians, are encouraged to open our hearts to God and to one another. God was in Christ reconciling the world to himself (2 Corinthians 5:19), therefore we are reconciled to one another. This is no small matter for Paul. This is the very heart of the gospel. This is not a flimsy philosophy, it is a way of life. Without it, God's grace is in vain.

We are ambassadors for Christ (5:20), entrusted with the message of reconciliation, announcing God's love and forgiveness so that we might live in peace with one another.

Reflect: What are some things you would like to put in order? Are any of them relationships? Where are you called to be an ambassador of God's love and peace?

Don't Lose Heart
2 Corinthians 4:13-5:1

Preparation

- Beforehand, everyone read all of 2 Corinthians in one sitting. Make note of the things that jump out at you and any questions that come to mind. Underline or highlight passages that have meaning to you.
- Read the Introduction in *A Heart for Reconciliation.*
- As you gather, share a meal together, or have snacks and drinks for 30 minutes before beginning the group gathering.

Gather

- Ask someone in your group to begin the group gathering with a prayer of thanks for the food and for the group.
- Share your name and some other interesting facts about yourself. Who invited you to this group? Why did you say yes?
- When was the last time you wrote a letter to someone by hand, on paper? What's the longest letter you've ever written?

Word

- For those who read 2 Corinthians beforehand, what were your impressions? What jumped out at you? What questions did the text raise for you?
- Have the group discuss some of the questions that came up. You will find many of the questions will be addressed in the daily devotional materials, and also in the background material found at: http://bishopmike.com/2-corinthians.
- Have someone in your group read 2 Corinthians 4:13-5:1 aloud. Listen for the word or phrase that grabs you the most.

- Share around the room the words or phrases the grabbed you the most.
- In what ways are our outer natures wasting away as we grow older? Did the young people in the group feel their outer natures are wasting away?
- In what ways is your inner nature being renewed daily?
- What might it mean to look to the things that are unseen? What are the important things in life that cannot be seen? Love, for example, is not a physical, tangible, touchable thing, and yet it is very important. What are some other invisible, spiritual aspects of life to which we look to be renewed?

Send

- What will you do this week to pay more attention to those unseen, spiritual aspects of life, so that your inner nature might be renewed daily? What would be most helpful to stay mindful of these things?
- As a group, commit to the daily readings, the weekly group gatherings and weekly worship.
- Confirm your dates and places for the group gatherings, and decide who will bring food. Are there childcare needs?
- Take a moment for the group to share prayer requests.
- Close with a group prayer or the Lord's Prayer.

After:

- Read a chapter of *A Heart for Reconciliation* and half of a chapter of 2 Corinthians each day.
- Set aside time for daily silent prayer.
- Your pastor will be preaching on these five study texts. Think about the connections between what you hear in worship and your group conversation.

A Heart for Reconciliation Group Gathering 2

New Creation
2 Corinthians 5:6-10, (11-13), 14-17

Preparation
- Beforehand, read the first 3-5 chapters of 2 Corinthians, a bit each day, and the first six chapters of *A Heart for Reconciliation*, one each day. Take Sunday off of reading, and worship instead. Underline or highlight things that jump out at you and write any questions that come to mind.
- As you gather, share a meal together, or have snacks and drinks for 30 minutes before beginning the group gathering.

Gather
- Ask someone in your group to begin the group gathering with prayer.
- Share with the group how your reading and prayer went this week.
- Describe a time you embarked upon a new job or a new career, or moved to a new town. How did it feel to start over, anew.

Word
- What were your impressions of the first three or four chapters of 2 Corinthians? What jumped out at you? What questions surfaced for you?
- Have someone in your group read 2 Corinthians 5:6-17 aloud, or split it up among group participants willing to read. Listen for the word or phrase that grabs you the most.
- Share around the room the word or phrase that grabbed you the most.
- What might it means to walk by faith, rather than by sight? What might Paul mean? What does it mean to live by faith?
- What is the opposite of faith? Doubt? Fear? Despair?

- In what ways might you be becoming a new creation? In what ways would you like to become a new creation?

Send

- What will you do this week to walk by faith, and not by sight?
- As a group, make plans to do some kind of service project together.
- Take a moment for the group to share prayer requests.
- Close with the group prayer or the Lord's Prayer.

After

- Daily, read a chapter of *A Heart for Reconciliation* and half of a chapter of 2 Corinthians.
- Set aside time for daily silent prayer.
- Your pastor will be preaching on these five study texts. Think about the connections between what you hear in worship and your group conversation.

Open Heart
2 Corinthians 6:1-13

Preparation
- Beforehand, read through chapter six or seven of 2 Corinthians, half a chapter a day, and through chapter 12 of *A Heart for Reconciliation*. Underline or highlight things that jump out at you and write any questions that come to mind.
- As you gather, share a meal together, or have snacks and drinks for 30 minutes before beginning the group gathering.

Gather
- Begin with a group prayer in which each person gives thanks for one or two things in their lives.
- Share with the group how your reading and prayer went this week.
- Tell the group about someone in your life who you would describe as having an "open heart." What are his or her characteristics? What impact has this person had on you?

Word
- What were your impressions of chapters 3-6 of 2 Corinthians? Share anything you highlighted or underlined. Discuss questions that emerged for group members.
- Have someone in your group read 2 Corinthians 6:1-13 aloud. Listen for the word or phrase that grabs you the most.
- Share around the room the word or phrase that grabbed you the most.
- Throughout 2 Corinthians, Paul references a former "letter of tears," and someone who has done something wrong. If the Corinthians are willing to forgive, he is too. Paul sees reconciliation as part of salvation. The time is now. When

you have a conflict, why is it good to reconcile as soon as possible? What are the risks of delaying?

- Reading all of Paul's hardships, did they surprise you? Why does he mention them?
- What does Paul mean when he says their hearts are open to the Corinthian church?
- Why does he mean when he asks them to open their hearts too?

Send

- Are there those in your life to whom you need to open your heart?
- As a group, make plans to do some kind of service project together.
- Take a moment for the group to share prayer requests.
- Close with the group prayer or the Lord's Prayer.

After

- Daily, read a chapter of *A Heart for Reconciliation* and half of a chapter of 2 Corinthians.
- Set aside time for daily silent prayer.

A Heart for Reconciliation Gathering 4

Eager Generosity
2 Corinthians 8:7-15

Preparation
- Beforehand, read through chapter nine of 2 Corinthians, half a chapter a day, and through chapter 18 of *A Heart for Reconciliation*. Underline or highlight things that jump out at you and write any questions that come to mind.
- As you gather, share a meal together, or have snacks and drinks for 30 minutes before beginning the group gathering.

Gather
- Begin with a group prayer in which each person gives thanks for someone who has given them a lot in this life.
- Share with the group how your reading and prayer went this week.
- Last week you shared a name of someone with an "open heart." This week, tell the group about someone in your life who you would describe as having a "big heart."

Word
- What were your impressions of chapters 7-9 of 2 Corinthians? Share anything you highlighted or underlined. Discuss questions that emerged for group members.
- Have someone in your group read 2 Corinthians 8:1-15 aloud. Listen for the word or phrase that grabs you the most.
- Share around the room the word or phrase that grabbed you the most.
- This is a bold move. Paul has been begging for reconciliation, now, in chapters 8 and 9, he asks them to make good on a financial pledge they made to the poor in Jerusalem. Do you think this will help or hurt his plea for reconciliation? How might it bond them?

- What effect might Paul's boasting about the offering of the Macedonian church have?
- What do you think Paul means in verse 12, "If there is eagerness, give according to what you have, not what you don't have..."

Send

- What do you believe about giving? What were you taught as a child?
- Do you plan your giving? If you're willing, share what kinds of organizations to which you give.
- Carry out your service project together if you have not already done so.
- Take a moment for the group to share prayer requests, then close with prayer.

After

- Consider your giving for the coming year. Plan it out. Talk to your family about it.
- Finish *A Heart for Reconciliation* and 2 Corinthians.
- Set aside time for daily silent prayer.

Powerful Weakness

2 Corinthians 12:2-10

Preparation

- Beforehand, read chapters 10-13 of 2 Corinthians, half a chapter a day, and through the end of *A Heart for Reconciliation*. Underline or highlight things that jump out at you and write any questions that come to mind.
- As you gather, share a meal together, or have snacks and drinks for 30 minutes before beginning the group gathering.

Gather

- Begin with a group prayer in which each person prays for someone in need.
- Share with the group how your reading and prayer went this week.
- Can you share something that happened to you 14 years ago?
- Share a time in which you were weak, hurting, wounded, in the hospital, or grieving.

Word

- What were your impressions of chapters 10-13 of 2 Corinthians? Share highlights and questions. Could you feel the different tone of this part of the letter?
- Have someone in your group read 2 Corinthians 12:2-20 aloud. Listen for the word or phrase that grabs you the most.
- Share around the room the word or phrase that grabbed you the most.
- What tells you that Paul is actually talking about himself in this passage?
- Have you ever had a hard-to-explain, mystical experience?

- Paul may be describing a physical malady. We know Paul had an eye problem, from Galatians. Paul could be describing a sin he can't overcome. What would you guess Paul's thorn in the flesh is?
- Why do you suppose God does not deliver Paul from his "thorn in the flesh?"
- What might Paul mean in verse 9, ""My grace is sufficient for you, for power is made perfect in weakness."?

Send

- God often uses our weakness, our brokenness, our soft spot, to open our hearts and also minister to others. In what ways have your thorns in the flesh been a blessing to others?
- When have you experienced God working powerfully through weakness, rather than force?
- How has this group been for you? What have been the highs and lows?
- Consider continuing with your group after a short break. Choose another study. Would you want to meet weekly? Every other week? What might be the benefits? Who else might you include? Close with prayer.

Appendix:

Background Material and Using *A Heart for Reconciliation* as a Series

This walk through 2 Corinthians can be used as series in your congregation, or simply with your small group.

Background Material on 2 Corinthians and the five small group test can be found at http://bishopmike.com/2-corinthians/.

When used as a series there are three parts:

1. **Daily devotions** – Reading daily from *A Heart for Reconciliation* and from selected passages in 2 Corinthians.
2. **Weekly Bible study** – Go through the small group discussion questions below.
3. **Sunday worship** – Background material and sermon helps are available at http://bishopmike.com/2-corinthians/.

Here are the weekly themes

Don't Lose Heart
Pentecost 2B: June 7, 2015 – **2 Corinthians 4:13-5:1** – So we do not lose heart. Though our outer nature is wasting away, our inner nature is being renewed daily.

New Creation Pentecost 3B: June 14 – **2 Corinthians 5:6-10, (11-13), 14-17** – If anyone is in Christ, there is a new creation. We walk by faith and not by sight, at home in the body and away from the Lord.

Open Heart
Pentecost 4B: June 21 – **2 Corinthians 6:1-13** – Now is the acceptable time; now is the day of salvation. We have endured beatings, riots, hunger, imprisonment…

Eager Generosity
Pentecost 5B: June 28 – **2 Corinthians 8:7-15** – The offering for the poor in Jerusalem. Now as you excel in everything—in faith, in speech, in knowledge, in utmost eagerness, and in our love for you—so we want you to excel also in this generous undertaking.

Powerful Weakness
Pentecost 6B: July 5 – **2 Corinthians 12:2-10** – Paul's out of body experience, and his thorn in the flesh. My grace is sufficient for you, for my power is made perfect in weakness.

Prepare

Prepare by recruiting small group hosts, who will open their home. Some groups may meet at your church, but home groups have a higher rate of welcoming friends. Small group hosts need only open their home, offer snacks (or coordinate others to do so) and ask the discussion questions that are provided.

More thoughts on putting together small groups can be found at http://bishopmike.com/2-corinthians/ by clicking on "Launching Small Groups."

Make a sheet for each group, on which people can sign up and put it in your meeting area. Announce it every Sunday for a month or two beforehand. Ask hosts to recruit for their groups. Have one gathering for hosts before the series begins. On the last day of the series, consider having a party for the whole congregation, or for all group participants.

Then watch people grow as they engage Scripture.

Made in the USA
Lexington, KY
07 May 2015